I Now Know
Who I AM!

Leavitt Peak Press

ISBN: 978-1-969865-98-5 (sc)
ISBN: 978-1-969865-99-2 (e)

Rev. date: 02/09/2026

I Now Know
Who I AM!

DR. TRUTH

I looked into the mirror
To see what I would see.
I saw someone I didn't know
looking back at me.

At first it really scared me,
For I truly Could not deny
That face I'd always seen was mine.
Yet I wondered, *Who am I?*

I knew I had to *know the truth.*
But where, oh where, could it be?
Then I thought to myself, *Oh, I know.*
I'll go to the library!

There were so many books there,
yet I still hoped to find
the book that was right for me.
The one that would set me on the right path
to find my **true...identity.**

"Who am I?" I asked myself.
Right now I just must know!
To be all that I am called to be
and to go wherever I am meant to go.

I knew I had to know the truth,
but where, oh where, could it be?
Then I found it. Oh yes, I found it as I read the
B-I-B-L-E.

Now I know what "thus says the Lord"
about my identity.
Now I know **who I AM**,
and what is my life's destiny.

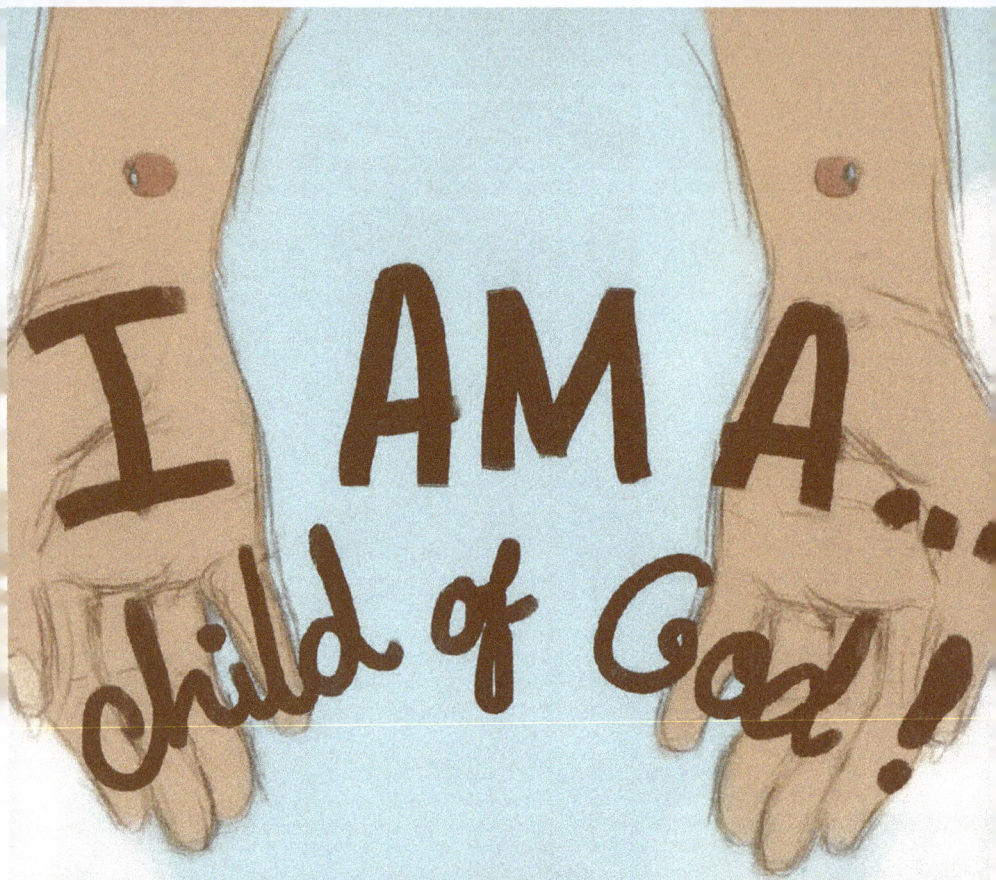

I AM a child of GOD!
I am in His family.
He is the King of kings
so that makes me royalty!

I am the head and not the tail,
above only and not below.
I am blessed to **be a blessing**
even to those I do not know.

I am the seed of Abraham,
an heir of God, and a joint-heir with Christ.
He died for me so that I could live for Him.
I'd say, "That's very nice!"

I am made in His image; after his likeness,
for all the world to see.
I am a **spirit** with a **soul** who lives is **a body**.
Like my father, **I Am a TRINITY!**

When my Heavenly Father speaks,
there is power in HIS Words.
He is "the God" who calls me "a god."
🌈 Psalms 82:6
And in my mouth has placed HIS Words.
🌈 Jeremiah 1:9

I now speak those words with boldness
because I know who I am, you see.
I am a child of "The Most High GOD"!
It is my destiny **to reign with Him for all eternity**.

So now when I pray
I know I will be heard,
for I pray to my Father
by speaking His word.

And now I know without a doubt
how to have all I want and need,
for I am a sower of the Word,
that incorruptible seed!

Our Father who art in heaven, hallowed be thy name.

Thy kingdom come, Thy will be done. . .

Matthew 6: 9-15

I am all that the Word says I am!
I can be what-ever it says I am to be.
I can have everything it says I can have.
This is my forever destiny!

I can do all things through Christ.
He's the one who strengthens me.
I am never alone,
for He is always with me!

Even when I am sad
and feeling all alone,
I am always on His mind
because I am His own.

I am in Him, and He is in me.
We now walk together daily
as one new spirit...who others can see
living in love, peace, and harmony.
My life is not my own,
for it has been bought with a price.
🌈 I Corinthians 6:19-20
I am redeemed from the curse.
🌈 Galatians 3:13
I have received a new life!

Now that life which I once knew
will never be again.
For I've been given power to change things.
The power of...His name!

Now I know what I must do,
and why I must be heard,
why I have to know who I am.
It's so I can spread The Word.

For many are lost and lonely today
in this very dark world where we live.
And many are searching for answers
that...Only GOD...can give.

I AM TAKING THE GOSPEL THE TOP OF THE WORLD, AND ALL THE WAY AROUND IT

But as I get to know me
by looking up above,
I also get to know Him–
Our Heavenly Father and His love.

I am the product of this love.
I am loved, **For HE IS LOVE!**
And as he is...so am I...in this earth,
reflecting His glory through my awesome rebirth!

This is who... "I AM"
and forever more **shall be!**
Never again to be bound
to a false identity!

And if in your heart
you believe this is true,
then right now at this very moment
this is what you should do:

SAY; *"Father in heaven, please forgive me*
and make my life brand-new.
Renew your holy spirit within me
so that I can have, be, and do...
all that You have said that I Am,
as I live my new life... through YOU! AMEN."